BOLD KIDS

Light Energy

CHILDREN'S PHYSICS BOOK

No part of this book may be reproduced or used in any way or form or by any means whether electronic or mechanical, this means that you cannot record or photocopy any material ideas or tips that are provided in this book.
Copyright 2022

All images in this book have been reproduced with the knowledge and prior consent of the artists concerned, and no responsibility is accepted by producer, publisher, or printer for any infringement of copyright or otherwise, arising from the contents of this publication.

Did you know that light has a wavelength? It's made up of tiny particles known as photons, and the wavelengths of light change its direction when they travel through different materials. This is because different materials slow down the speed of light.

The refractive index of glass is 1.5, so it slows down light by over 124,000 miles per second. Water and air have a refractive index of 1.000.

When you look into a mirror, the atoms in the mirror absorb the light that comes from the face of the person who looks into it. As a result, the atoms become excited by the energy of the light that comes into them, and then they give out new photons.

These new light particles then travel back to the original object. The process is called 'refracting'. A refractive index is a measure of how much a material slows down light.

A great way to teach kids about light is to make a project about it. They can build a model for the Sun or a model of the Milky Way, or they can create a 3-D model with a hologram.

When they are finished, they can build a light-up from a photon, and then watch it move. This process can be repeated over again!

Light is the most abundant source of energy in the universe. It's the most powerful star in the sky, so it radiates an incredible amount of energy every single day. It travels through different mediums, like air, water, and glass, and has an incredible impact on the Earth.

You can see light in a mirror, and your eyes can see it in a plant. If you can imagine a photon moving through a plant, you can imagine that light is traveling in the exact same way.

Light is a form of energy. It travels through the air, and stars give off light. It is a very small part of the electromagnetic spectrum, but it has a profound impact on our lives.

The energy from light is essential for life, and plants are the biggest source of light. It gives us a sense of sight. And as you can see, light is a fundamental part of our universe.

Light is a type of energy. It's a type of electromagnetic radiation that can be detected by the human eye. The sun gives off an incredible amount of light, and this energy can affect the earth's surface.

However, it doesn't travel as fast as it does in air, so its effects are not as obvious. In the same way, light is also an important source of food. Hence, you can learn about light through this book.

The biggest source of light is the sun. Although the Sun is millions of miles away, it transfers an amazing amount of energy to Earth. The speed of light is 300,000 kilometres per second.

This energy affects all kinds of things on Earth, from plants to stars. They can use this energy to produce food and grow. And they can even create their own lights! It's amazing what the sun can do.

We have a lot of uses for light. The human eye can see and hear images. We can see objects in the dark, and the sun is our main source of light. The human eye can't make it, but the camera helps us see.

The light we see is also used for other things, like writing. Moreover, light can be converted into thermal energy by plants. In the end, a burning candle can transform light into heat.

Ingram Content Group UK Ltd.
Milton Keynes UK
UKHW050053130623
423325UK00008B/62

8 Unidades

Letterland

Pat, pat!
and other stories

These **Phonics Readers** give children the satisfaction of reading whole books as soon as they know a few letter sounds. The imaginative, decodable stories gradually introduce new phonic elements and build on the vocabulary from previous stories in a clear and measurable progression.

Stories in this book:
Sss!
Pat, pat!

Focus on:
s as in <u>s</u>un, **a** as in <u>a</u>dd
t as in <u>t</u>ap, **p** as in <u>p</u>en

Phonics Readers - Red Series

See our full range at **www.letterland.com**